Jim Johnson | *One Morning In June: Selected Poems*

Jim Johnson

One Morning In June

Selected Poems

Red Dragonfly Press

   ISBN 978-1-945063-33-6 paper

   Library of Congress Control Number: 2020934447

Acknowledgments

A Field Guide To Blueberries (North Star Press, 1992); *Wolves* (New Rivers Press, 1993); *The Coop Label* (Dovetailed Press, 2005); *Driving Gravel Roads* (Red Dragonfly Press, 2009); *The First Day Of Spring In Northern Minnesota* (Red Dragonfly Press, 2012); *Yoik* (Red Dragonfly Press, 2015); *Text For Our Nomadic Future* (Red Dragonfly Press, 2018); *Fire Speaks Our Words* (Carlton County Historical Society, 2018)

Cover Photo: *Disestablish* 54"x42" sumi ink & guache on paper 2017
   artist Crit Streed

Designed and typeset at Red Dragonfly Press
   using Warnock Pro digital type and Rialto

Printed in the United States of America
   on 30% recycled stock
   by BookMobile, a 100% wind-powered company

Published by Red Dragonfly Press
   P. O. Box 98
   Northfield, MN 55057

For more information and additional titles visit our website
   www.reddragonflypress.org

CONTENTS

WOLVES

THE COOP LABEL

TEXT FOR OUR NOMADIC FUTURE

FIRE SPEAKS OUR WORDS

Index of Titles and First Lines

About the Author

A FIELD GUIDE TO BLUEBERRIES

I give to you:
       small brook trout from unnamed brooks
       mushrooms
       full moons
       the contents of a grouse's craw:
              51 clover leaves
              34 alder cones
               9 twigs with deerfoot buds
               1 piece quartzite
and blueberries.

WHEN PICKING BLUEBERRIES AN EARLY START IS OF UTMOST IMPORTANCE

In Lake County along the road
in a slough
in the early morning still
silted in the still of night, a mist coming off
when a moose—humped darkness that arced
into dark water (as I stopped the pickup truck)
suddenly
rose out of the slough
upslurping all silence—an antlered head huge
great clumps of distant timber remembered
earth clinging to the roots, its eyes large
bullheadedly round, not yet of daylight, and
its mouth nonchalantly moving stems to
dangle
lilypads already turned lavender.

IN BLUEBERRY COUNTRY

Sign by the road: *Minnows, Crawlers, Leeches.*
I remember: fish bite best when the mermaid's tail turns blue.

HEADING NORTH

Through the pine shadow
a crow flies
parallel the dusty road.

WHERE THEY GROW, HOW SERIOUSLY TAKEN

In a clearing cleared by loggers, blueberries
acres and acres of
blueberries, each one a different color.

WHEN TO PICK

It's best to pick on a clear day with some wind,
           a high blue sky.
Still humid days are the worst.
Even on a dry day black flies buzz your hands
                              buzz your arms
                              buzz your face, any exposed skin.
As you pick you brush your face
                   brush your arms
                   brush your hands between every bunch
you pick picking up a way of life, if you must know, is not your life.
Then
and only then, if you must not, it is.

BLACKFLIES — SMALL HUMPBACKED GNATS NOT
CONFINED TO THE NORTH COUNTRY, BREED IN FLOWING
WATER, LAY EGGS ON STICKS, ROCKS PROJECTING INTO
WATER, LARVAE CLINGING TO OBJECTS (OLD SHOES, BEER
CANS) IN WATER FROM WHICH THEY GATHER FOOD WITH
SET OF MOTILE BRUSHES AROUND MOUTH, SPIN WEB-LIKE
POCKETS UNDERWATER, AND PUPATE — NOW

About your neck
        your ears
like an old woman with knitting and questions
occasionally one gets in.

BLUER THAN A BOTTLE OF THE GREAT DOCTOR KILMER'S
SWAMP ROOT, BLACKER THAN THE PARTICLES OF NIGHT,
BRIGHTER THAN BEAR'S HAIR, CUBS HUNG FROM HER
SUMMER

The true blueberry is
heaven and earth
      the four winds and dark water
yet it tastes
of nothing.

ANOTHER STEP FORWARD

Walking through the brush once logged over, now
grown up with waist high cover
I hear something ahead.
I stop. Then silence.
I go on,
hear it again. Again I stop. And again
silence. I go on
as the other end of the fir log
I am standing on
takes another step forward.

WEAR STURDY SHOES, LONG SLEEVED SHIRT BUTTONED
TO THE TOP, LONG PANTS, AND A HAT, AND DO NOT OIL
BOOTS WITH OIL OF PREY

Close to the road and low to the ground and
hard to find
the stems tangled with sticks, dried grass, and
for a long time see nothing, nothing to pick, and
having the time to think
having the time to think
turn over and over another bush.

THE NAMES LOGGERS GIVE TO THE TREES OFTEN DIFFER

Because loggers often built their own roads
the law didn't apply to them.
They brought their children up
believing. I remember when
I drove a narrow
gravel road and
met a logging truck doing 50 miles per hour
no room to get over. Somehow
I got by.
The road rose. Sunlight slanted
through the pines and dust.
I thought of having come through
one life into another.
So many questions. Now
the stones no longer listen.

LAND LEASED FROM INDIANS LONG AGO LOGGED OVER,
SURVEYED INTO TOWNSHIPS, DRAWN INTO SECTIONS,
THEN QUARTERED AND SOLD TO IMMIGRANTS

Far to the north where summer is
an illusion we live on
I find bottles broken into lavender pieces of glass
a wash basin
its bottom rusted out and
cans (only one a Hamms is recognizable). These too
are seeds buried in this earth.

They cut timber in Isabella Minnesota.
Sell gas, bait. Minnows only.
No leeches or ice. Work on
skidders. Saturdays off.
Come Monday it takes a long time
to spit snooze, rub it into
the ground, look at a
chainsaw. How the blade
is shaped like a beaver's tail.
Around the blade are teeth.
The body usually a color like
yellow but the same
size. To skin it out
simply unscrew a nut behind
the handle. Around here
some people think they are a nuisance.
Cutting down the trees, damming
the streams. Where the meadow grass
narrows, a point of firs.
The waters backed up like twilight
are the stained glass windows
of the log cathedral. Artisans
worked for years piecing together
pieces of Jesus feeding the multitudes
loaves and fishes. Men will lay down
a foot or leg before a chainsaw.
Beaver men lived their lives
for someone else's hat.

CLINTONIA

False blueberries I call them
a single berry like a blue lightbulb on a stem
growing out of three lily-like leaves
growing so near
blueberries I always find a few
in my bucket after picking.
They taste bitter, maybe poisonous
maybe not. The true with the false
the false with the true, without order
and in reverse order, hidden
as much as possible. A separateness
beginning with a name.

THE CONIFERS ARE IDENTIFIED BY NEEDLE-LIKE LEAVES

In the slanting light between the trees
a fir branch moving, moving
like a bird's wing. It is a bird's wing.

THE TASTE IS EVERYTHING

How would it be to have a blueberry contest
to see who could bring in the biggest blueberry?
You couldn't, someone would bring in
a domestic blueberry
say it was wild and
you couldn't tell
unless
of course, you tasted it.

THE BARK: DARK, THICK, DEEPLY FURROWED WITH BROAD RIDGES COMPOSED OF CLOSELY PRESSED PURPLE TINGED SCALES

Like the winter hardened faces
that go out onto the ice in early November
when the ice is thin
no snow and so clear
maybe they see the faces of the children
the ones who died, who were too bright.
Now they are the ones who cut down the pines.
You never see them weep
or look up too long
before they get out of the way. The Indians used
the inner bark for food, an ingredient in cough syrup.

SEEING

No wind.
In the clearing
cleared by loggers
a hawk perched on
a dead fir
the top broken
off, seeing only
movement, seeing being
the only movement.

INSIDE EACH BERRY A THOUSAND SEEDS LIKE THE ENDS OF
POPPLE LOGS CUT AND STACKED, THE PITH DEVELOPING
LIKE A FETUS, IN EACH LOG A DIFFERENT SHAPE

The wolf scat I found in March
on the trail of crusted snow
was nothing more than
excreted brown fur. A few days
a south wind and
the snow hardened by premature melt
the scat dry out
whiten
and come apart each
individual hair seeping into the ground
                        like roots.

REASONS WHY THERE IS A BLUEBERRY GOD

I once brought berries and small trout to
an old woman who lived alone. She made
me coffee. She was herself full of grounds.
I said to her *If you think the ice won't hold
even in January when three feet thick, you
are sure to find a spring hole.* And she said
to me, *Because of where they are located,
some thermometers are optimists. Only
when the sky closes its eyes,* I said to her,
does snow fall. Dogs run faster in moonlight,
she said to me, *when the shapes of tall pines
turn.* And I knew, *Too far east is west.*

ALL PART OF THE COMMUNITY WHERE PLANTS AND ANIMALS LIVE

Pull it through your fingers.
It is long and thin a red fox hair
with the slightest bit of
fox skin at one end
and tapering to nothing
at the other.
Pull it across your nostrils.
Feel your back begin to hackle
paws begin to twitch
something wild
something sniffing
sniffing sniffing for more.

IN ISABELLA MINNESOTA I HAVE FOUND CRYSTALS OF DIRTY
SNOW UNDER A LOG, EVEN IN JULY

And blueberries
     green blueberries red blueberries ripe blueberries
     blue blueberries blueberries blue as Finland blue
     black blueberries black blue blueberries white spotted
     blueberries withered white blueberries thousands and
     thousands of blueberries—each one the end of summer.

HOW BLUEBERRIES ARE MEASURED

At home
the small red dots along your arms, behind your ears
above your sock line, your waistline, in the corner of
your eye—small red dots where blackflies got in
     small red dots about the same size
          as blueberries not quite ripe.

AS IDENTIFIED BY SOFT BLUE NEEDLES FIVE TO A BUNCH

When I touch the ends of your hairs with my tongue
it might be the wind licking the treetops.

DRIVING HOME WHILE THE MOON REPEATS ITSELF NOT
FAR FROM ISABELLA MINNESOTA

The August moon above the trees
not quite full like a Canadian dollar
in and of itself now spent
shining down on a last tangent of lilypads.

AFTERWARDS

In the kitchen with two buckets of blueberries
I drink wine from a water glass
and feel the swelling
behind my ears
along my hairline. I close
my eyes and see
see only blueberries and know
how the blackflies fertilize the blueberries that
there is a wisdom in all things
                                        except mosquitos.

No one else can pick them for you. You must put
all—homegrown tomatoes, the chance of frost,
more stovewood—aside and go. Suffer the blackflies
and mosquitos. Go out onto the woods. Once near
Bear River I actually saw a bear run across the highway.
Only later, much later, did I come to believe it was,
it ever will be, and that that is why we make pies.

☾ WOLVES

The way things are
in the middle of every field
on every homestead
a tree
usually a white birch
left only for the birds.
Midday
a man wipes his brow
unfolds his lunch
and takes a long slow
swallow of spring water
in the shade of the uncut
tree. The young
like branches
are reaching out
going to town leaving
home, there is a girl
a job in the cities, then
who knows
there are no more
letters, only the fresh cut of
hay rising up
the sound a baler makes
continuing on, and
the way things are
a tree
left only for the birds.

So the young man took the old man
whose hair was then white as the foam
        on the lakeshore on a windy day
showed him the backhoe
how it ate great mouthful after mouthful
of earth and roots and clay.

Did the young man know the origin of iron.
Did he know the old man cut trees and
        built the house, the log house.
Did he know the land was as a woman
        dark as the bark of trees on a rainy day.
How the old man plowed the land
        piled rocks, dug a well.

Does a young man look past the end of the road
        at the boughs of the balsam fir.
How the boughs become the trees.
How the stems become the trunks, the flat needles
        the boughs, the boughs shaped
like the slopes of mountains.
How the roots go down deeper than the cold.
How the water tastes of iron.

THE BACK ROADS

Out on the back roads
driven only by road hunters
and others who want only to know
where these roads go,
out on the end of a long-necked pole
anchored to a post or milk pail
filled with cement
an occasional mailbox.
Each one
moose-jawed to open and close
take in and spit out
the news of the day. A red flag
goes up if something to say.
On each is painted a name
like Heinonen.   If you go far enough
you never see anyone.
It is only the balsams that
come out to the road
wanting to know
who drives these roads.

SUNDOGS

We know neither
the secret of creation
nor why dogs sleep
on chairs or couches
with knitted throws
around a woodstove
or in the sunlight
their paws chinking in
a part of a life
that wasn't. Once
a man came from
beyond the black spruce
to tell me a chipmunk
passed away. He
didn't have anything else to say.
One of the dogs
one with a black mark
over one eye
woke up when he arrived
barked once, then
rolled over. The first of
January. Minus twelve
degrees. On the window
suddenly so much sunlight.

In a yellowed photograph I am five years old and standing beside a huge fish, a northern pike. Its mouth is slightly open like enormous pliers. There is a rope strung through the trap-like gills from which the fish hangs from a willow limb I used to climb out onto. When I asked, my father said the fish was twenty-six pounds and fourteen ounces and that he would have caught that fish except one Hjalmer Maki wouldn't stop the boat when my father yelled to him to stop the boat that he had hooked a big fish, but the lake was too rough and Hjalmer Maki wouldn't shut the motor off. My father must have fought that fish for half an hour while Hjalmer Maki and his Johnson three-horse kept on puttputtputt into the big wind until finally the big fish got off. For weeks Hjalmer Maki trolled alone before he caught the big fish and my father swore it was from the same spot he had hooked his big fish so it must have been the same fish. Now every summer the lake turns green.

HEAD CHEESE

We eat the heart
      the throat
      the brains, sliced a mosaic remains
we use all of the animal.

We break open the bones
lick the narrow marrow
eat the very tongue, and
use all of the animal.

Skins stretched for drying
sinew split for thread
bones carved, then worshipped
we use all of the animal.

Knife twisted into the heart
blood flowing into the stomach
now removed in moonlight
we use all of the animal.

Fresh blood in pancakes
first milk in cheese
a little *viili*
we use all of the animal.

There are scratch marks on trees
the bushes trampled
black shit
pitted with chokecherry seeds.

What we are we are:
Finns
Italians
Serbs and Swedes. What we are

we are. We use all
all of the animal.

A reply made by an Ojibwe guide when told by a judge he couldn't use his snowmobile in the Boundary Waters Canoe Area anymore.

Just off the country road
tarpaper
nailed down with strips
a ladder to the roof where
the roof was shingled years ago
bleached antlers nailed above
a sliding corrugated door.

Deep in grass out back
cars pickup trucks bodies
rusted with sin and without
wheels. On a popple log
tripod
a chain, the ground
around engine-block black.

A rusted bucket
bolts and nails
a broken chair
an old shirt hung out on a pump
sleeves limp in the wind
that crossed the field

the next field
green as after rain
where two deer, a doe and fawn
stand out of the evening. There
they will always be.

WOLVES

1

Morning
and not a whimper.
The moon chill
had scattered frost across the near fields.

When I found the dog dead
dead at the end of the frozen chain
I blew blew blew
until the ghost entered the clasp and
unfroze it at last
as if my breath could bring back
life. It couldn't.
The throat ripped
the abdomen tore open
the dog was dead.

Unclasped
what remained
was of the wolves
fur
flesh and
bone
          warm yet as the stars
over a bent-over earth, white with fright.

2

Against the chill
I loaded the woodstove,

pulled on wool melton pants
pockets that sagged with
cartridges
matches and wire
a cache of head cheese and biscuit
a jar of gonads.

Then
looked long
into the oiled gleam of rifling.
Night after night
raven after raven
scavenged the reddened flesh.
the crushed bone.
Furborn or not
this was ancient hatred—
a bullet was light
at the end of the blueblack night.

This was tempered
made in the U.S.A.
steel
eight cartridges
open and closed
one was for the chamber—
a dog lay dead.

3

For a moment
among the dark humus dripping
roots
strewn with

bones feathers fur
here where sniff was history
I prepared
teeth to each
paw pad and claw.

4

The trees had surrendered
their leaves.
I walked

all day against the wind. The sky clouded over.
No sign of wolves. Eight dogs were dead. If only
I had waited
each night with a rifle
waited
        for eyes knotting the shadows of birches
my own eyes splintered open
by death smell and deer hair blown across
an April five years ago
a deer unable to get up onto
the blood splashed crust, flesh and hair
snapped from its broken down flanks
then ears bristling
fierce lined eyes and teeth turned
at me.
        I walked away. This death becoming
the moment of my own, the dusk upon me
I turned
in wet clay and
track on my track
a wolf!

a four-toed ace of spades
a track as large
as nearly half my own.

5

Traps.
One Oedipus Koski
a wolfer
and I tried traps—
the civilized #14 Newhouse
buried for weeks
boiled in bark water
smeared in tallow, all
to give a black odor.

We set each
with a five-foot chain
and grapple
near a tainted bait
covered with leaves, dried grass.
We waited.

6

I waited.
On still cloudless nights
complete with moon
I heard them howl
that low
louder
ever melancholy howl that
hackled the hair along my back.

At first at one end of the frozen lake
howling, then
at the other end
howling howling
near the point and across
howling howling the unchained howling.

7

It was thirty-one degrees below zero
the night a Finn woman
looked out and saw
nothing but the stars, yet she knew
        a massive skull
            its pelage thick and
        nearly white
was there, where
in the morning
there were no tracks.

8

Wolves are seldom seen
yet always there—
deer hair
crushed bone
blood streaked April snow.

9

The rafters of the barn are
chinked with sunlight.
I watch the sky, the laws
the rivers

flow into backwaters. In the evenings
I take out my teeth
the Winchester
always above the door.

10

It has come to this:
these entrails
set out
and covered with brush
where a wolf
once so distant
circles
in ever narrowing circles
a wolf that haunts the forest
a wolf seldom seen
                              yet always there
a wolf that howls within us
a wolf that leaves no tracks.

◖ THE COOP LABEL

In Lake County where deer trials only recently
           gave way to roads
someone drives. The light rain that has been falling
           stops
and the sun drives a wedge to open the sky to
           fir trees and fields.
Soon it will be dusk and the gravel will give way
           to blacktop.

Once as I drove County 4 a deer, antlers in velvet
           running along the side—my foot off
the gas pedal, my mind already on the brakes—turned
crashing into the side of the truck.
I stopped.
Looked at the deer's
belly on blacktop, legs struggling but not splintered
           or broken. No blood.
It got up, wobbly at first as if new born
           as indeed it was
and somehow became the alder across the road.

Now with the coming of dusk the road seems longer
           than life.
The brown needles of the dead fir tree reincarnate
           a deer in its June fur.
The humus clinging to an uprooted tamarack
           resurrects the legs and antlers of a moose.
The sod gets up a porcupine.

Nothing ever dies.
One thing gives was to another and becomes
      its shadow.
Day flows into night. The body crosses over
      and becomes the soul.

❦ DRIVING GRAVEL ROADS

Always stay in the middle, the edges may be soft, unless you are afraid of high-centering. Slow down on washboard curves and uphills. Watch out for sharp rocks and boards with nails. When meeting another vehicle pull over as far as possible and, if the road is extremely narrow, stop. Unless the other driver stops for you. If he does, as you pass him uncurl your right index finger from the steering wheel and move it slowly to the right, then return it just as slowly, and close it back down into its grip. Do not expect large trucks, like logging trucks, to get over for you. If you meet one on a curve and don't have enough room to pass, you must go off the road. Understand that this is the only possibility. The larger truck can easily and certainly will pull you out of the trees/swamp/stream you are now in. Enjoy the experience. This is where you want to be. I know if my own skin were peeled back I would find beetle tracks, deer trails, tote and gravel roads, as well as interstate highways and sky.

❧ THE FIRST DAY OF SPRING IN
NORTHERN MINNESOTA

Pine tar, all witch smell and pitch
raven colored to boot
rubbed with a rag
onto the bottoms of the skis and
heated with the slow roar of a blow torch.
Then grip wax all the way from Holmenkol
Norway in a round tin like film
rubbed and corked in. And paraffin
lids pried off
the tops of jelly jars with a knife
rubbed on the tips and tails.
Fast skis glazed like two tracks
through the snow covered birches
the sun setting pink
as skin
scrubbed clean
in the sauna. On the top bench
threw a dipper of water
onto the rocks. *Ja,* the steam hissed up.
Later sipped the whiskey. Ate hardtack
with pickled herring and wild strawberry jam
from jars without lids. And knew:

if tar, sauna, whiskey wouldn't work
it couldn't be fixed.

Making The Skis

Since your only inheritance is the love of
wood, clear waters, cold winters, and snow
what else could you do but make the skis—
take oak or birch boards, saw to
length (not to exceed your reach), plane
thinner at the tails (squared) and tips (carved
to a point like a church steeple), then
build a fire under a black kettle of water
bring to a boil and add
the skis the way those Italians
feed sticks of linquini, boiling only
until the tips soften enough
to bend, then
take them out to the woodpile,
pile logs around and over the tips
so they curve like the slight
smile when you look back
on your life, a life not unlike
one Jackrabbit Johannesson who
at the age of 104
said, *Use the skis in winter, the canoe
in summer.* Then

there is the canoe.

The Middle Of March

The nights below zero, but during the day the snow started to melt, its crust like fish scales, and come apart from the trees. It is such a long journey to leave the circle of earth, last year's grass and leaves. Yet when Violet Wentala's cow walked through the fence, she was old enough and thin enough not to fall break through the crust. When she walked across the field, the cow ran into the trees. Time, you know, waits for no one. Neither did Violet Wentala's cow. When she walked into the woods, the cow ran out onto the highway where—not so fast that the clock stopped running—old Axel Maki drove his new Chevrolet Impala down the icy road. Have you ever seen a cow flying? When Violet Wentala saw her cow flying over the car, she knew it was too late. She knew she who lives long sees much. In fact, now she thought she had seen everything. The cow flying, its legs out like wings, flying over the crusted snow, landing, skidding on its belly—right by Violet Wentala—its legs out, then down into the ditch they both went. Though she was old enough not to live with an old man, she let Axel Maki help her butcher the cow. Maybe she hadn't seen everything yet. That afternoon she had a lump on her head and two eyes darkened like the circles of earth around the trees. It was the middle of March.

What The Red Squirrel Left

A dog looking up a pine tree; a chattering, bristling like needles; snow melt and the first smell of earth; the scales of pine cones found on stumps, rocks, the sauna steps; bits of styrofoam scattered on the outhouse floor; in the shed, shredded pieces of toilet paper woven into the sooted bristles of the chimney brush; even whole pine cones stuffed into a hip boot

as a footnote to a past too often not the way I left it.

Tamarack Of The Boreal Forest

After all the ice in the bog
has finally melted (late May)
soft green needles burst forth
in tufts
from branches jagged
as this life in wet acidic soil, this life
where all summer
the tamarack dances
barefoot and
beaded with red cones. All summer
she dances on cranberry blossoms
Labrador tea and sphagnum mosses
in her green tufted gown
until
she changes, as she does, into
her finest golden needled gown
which soon, also as she does, lets fall
into the marsh grass and steps
steps out
exposing—suppose you never heard of
malt liquor or rode in a heavy Chevy or at the end of the road
turned on the radio—her long bare limbs
to the darkened caress of early winter.

Trail

I went early. I went in the rain. I walked.
Turned off the gravel road
but two ruts.
Duff and tufted grass. A few
lichen-covered rocks.
Fiddle-head ferns grown up
to claim no one had driven this far.
Seedlings started
up in the ruts. Wild strawberries
also in their blossom. Then
a windfall—rusted bark and needles
the color of a deer born this year—across
the way. Boughs hung low:
burled, gnarled branches like old men
who when we look would be gods
with beards so pale green
you wondered if they ever doubted. If
a wide grassy spot was once
a turnaround. If out the back
was a trail, a trail leading on.

Known Stomach Contents Of Northern Pike

Obviously smelt, ciscoes, alewives, sculpins, suckers, whitefish, sticklebacks, darters, shiners, chubs, perch, all minnows come to mind. Also crayfish, frogs, leeches. Small varmints such as red-backed voles, red squirrels, bats that came too close to the water. As well as nighthawks, blackducks, crows, even chickens. Other items include: open jackknife, crescent wrench, flattened tin cans, gold watch and chain, silver dollars, and rodeo belt buckles carelessly dropped, and, what's more, ankle bracelets, earrings either dropped or worn carelessly into the water. In fact, our mothers even told us, we were just boys jumping into those cold northern lakes without suits, *Always swim on our backs.*

Highway One

Between Finland and
Isabella is the straightest
road in the state. And
the roughest.
Originally a corduroy road
laid down by loggers
now, so far from
St. Paul, summer after
summer paved over frost
heaves and lowlands that drop
off into muck where least
water lilies thrive. Here the shadows
of moose browse the edges.
Here you could turn off onto any
intersecting gravel road so
narrow there is no right or left
and know: the taste of black
blueberries, road dust, brook
trout, cedar boughs, or early
September mornings when
the smell of woodsmoke
lingers
like a solitary howl.

To carve a paddle
cut down a spruce
limb and cut to length
when the scent peels
easily in May though
you will wear a crown
of black flies consider
how the hand flows into the
handle the way the hand flows
into the ax the way the ax flows
into the wood the way the water
flows into water consider too as
you paddle into the early morning
mergansers flying up from the next
oxbow the stream meandering now
flowing in all four directions alder
reaching over cattails and marsh
grass flattened out by beaver
runs your paddle resting across
the gunnels as you watch the
water dripping back into
water remember too to
carve a paddle study
a beaver's tail.

Moose tracks are often found
along the sides of gravel roads head-
ing due north through stands of red pine
maybe a few whites. Each track is really a pair.
Like two quarter moons, one moon and one reflec-
tion out on the lake when you awaken before dawn and
    walk out to the outhouse (there on the door, we don't

    know why, is another moon). Or like two graves side by
side sunken in the ground. Lives lived out on homesteads
before they were ever connected by these roads. Lives
lived out like the sad lyrics of a tango. Now all that
remain are these dance steps written down
along the sides of the gravels roads, until
they too step out into the woods.

For Charlie Mayo

Cut thin the strips of birch bark that pop
        off the trunk late in June. From the bark
cut out tiny birch bark people.
Stick beeswax onto their feet.
Open the snuff box filled with wood ticks
        found stuck to us all day
        walking the woods, looking for
        what we did not know. Now
stick the waxed feet of each birch bark person
        onto the back of a wood tick and
let go. You might
blow through a reed with pin holes
        played by your fingers. Then
watch the birch bark people dance
dance along the lichen covered rock
dance across the mossy stump
dance down the sauna steps.
Dance. Dance. Trying to coax our souls
        out of their secret hiding places
out into the woods. Into the world.

Music For The Cows

Farmers are practical people. All night
in the barn the radio on.
In their stalls the cows listening to
the music of their lives. The butterfat
the yield increasing.
Grain dust does its dance on the old radio.
Hard-bodied insects rise into the winged life
a great changing of clothes. Our bodies too
shed and we go out in only our souls.
The older we get the more we long for
a music without words. So much
is left behind. In the morning
the phone rings. It is a neighbor saying
the cows are in her flowers.

Have You Ever Seen A Raven

Have you ever seen a raven
circling above a kill
waiting its turn
like a plane over Ely airport
patiently
until the wolves had eaten their fill
then swooping in.
To locate a kill locate a raven.
To locate a raven locate a kill.
The last wolf snapped back
at the first raven
landing on the bloody flank. Then
the raven
eying the eye of the wolf
eying the eye of the raven
cackled
knowing what it is to eat raven.

Have you ever seen a raven
soaring over the snow covered pines
over powerlines.
Have you ever seen a raven
perched on a snowbank, on a protruding
hoof. Have you ever seen a raven
beside the highway
you were driving from one job
to another because the one didn't pay
enough and the other wouldn't last?

Woodpiles

Those who build
haystacks or second
homes, collect poems
salt and pepper shakers
barbed wire, molecular
theories; or shovel snow
would know. It is not
the splitting, iron-headed
whether wielding ax or maul
arcing through an October less
than infinite, slab after slab
kicking off the block
to a scattered ungrained
pause, waiting to be piled.
As with kindling, it is not
the long thin stick
after stick
split off by a sharp ax
a mind that requires
stone from time to time
but
a putting back.
Not merely a cairn or
correct placement
of the moon in a seam
of rock or world order
but a woodpile.

Wood piled between
two trees or stakes.
Wood piled the length of a yard.
Then another in the same
direction with a walkspace
between. Another piled another
length. Another and
then another.
Like buidings built from slabs
of stovewood laid out
between streets of grass.
Wood piled in the round, ends out.
Wood piled in a hexagon, grain out.
Wood piled for sure
against ever burning. A man
carrying an armload
stops on his way to the house
and puts down
his load to pick up a slab exactly
the right length
or shape
whether birch or ash or oak
and returns to the pile
looking for
that gap
he had so long neglected.
What then did the woman say?

Stories Are Told

In cairns. On an island in Lake Superior
outcropped rock scoured by surf
the swells rolling in
falling out. In the fall birch leaves
yellow. Once rocks were
piled like moons around a mother world
by sky people who conversed with spirits
aligned the small islands
with the stars rising, the lake trout
spawning on reefs.

In the pictographs on Hegman Lake. Painted on the granite
cliff with vermilion squeezed from berries. The man with
large hands is Wintermaker himself as he appeared suddenly
above in the December stars. With him a wolf or panther
with a star-clustered tail. And a moose with antler points the
stars. Three canoes of departed souls pass by. Then in March
the corresponding stars departed too to their summer lodges.

On rocks and cliffs throughout the North
rock polypoides tell, perhaps
in a more lyrical nature, the same story
of the stars
colliding, dividing into life.

₵ YOIK

Among the Saami/reindeer people
a yoik is used to calm a reindeer, a baby.
Build community. Cooperation. Travel to
the other world. Locate lost objects.
Find fish. Restore health. Express feelings.
A yoik is not so much a song as it is
the voice. It speaks to the land. Tells us
we are all connected.
What can we do now but yoik?

River otter slide, slide like a tributary of the river itself, slide
down the bank of melting March snow, slide
into the open water riffling like a refracted
wink between the edges of the bright ice. First one otter. Then
another otter. And otter after otter after otter.
Five otter slide down the bank, cutting through the crusted snow
leaving a track of melting mud, down the bank and
into the water gurgling between this ice and that ice, between
March and April. River otter slide, one
after another after another after another after another.
River otter, five river otter in all, slide
down the bank of sun-reflected snow
each like the river itself, slide then
into the river itself.

The moon is tied off yet to the morning sky
pale against the ragged treeline. Only there
is the raven's glare. The sky flowing above
like the river below
riffling into a slow pool
encrusted in ice, the river riffling
into open water where
there appears
like a log, a bewhiskered log
then another and another and another and another
an entire family of, not logs, but
of river otter, river otter now looking up at you
river otter alive and bewhiskered
as the coming spring. The sun ascending

the snow melting, dripping
drop by drop
off the yellow grass, sliding
down the muddy bank and dropping
drop by drop by dew-wop drop
into the river and
becoming a tongue of the river
a riff here, a riffle there, each drop blending
into the a-cappella current,
into the scat-singing river, dropping like a family of
river otter sliding down the bank
otter after otter after otter after otter after otter
sliding into the singing river and becoming
each one the river itself.

The pine martin stars
in the dream of dark brown
almost black
a dream as dark as stonefly nymphs
under river rocks, dark as
the inside of wet branches
after days of rain
as black spruce roots growing
in low ground
tamarack-edged bog
red spoonleaf peat moss
turning into muskeg
roots built on roots, where
brook trout fin and loonshit
grabs your paddle
your foot
and pulls you in-
to acidic water, water
as dark as winter
below zero winter
nights dark as winter is long
and then
one day in March
the sun, a warm wind
the snow receding around the tall pines
revealing rusted needles
and duff, and
on a limb of one of the pines
a pine marten--
dark furred, cute
as a comma

scurrying along a branch. Then
you smell
the earth, the duff, the pines
as if for the first time
and awaken from the long dark dream.

TWINFLOWERS

A pair of white flowers so small
       you wouldn't notice if not the first
          to bloom.

A pair of small flowers so white
       like two left-over snowflakes
         on stems.

A woman
driving a Toyota Corolla
on Highway One
between Finland and
Isabella saw
a cow moose beside
the road, slowed
down, looked
ahead and saw
a bull moose charging her
the Toyota, hitting
the grill and bouncing
up and onto the hood
window glass
breaking, moose falling
to the side of the blacktop
bleeding into the club
moss, trout lilies, horsetail
and muck. After
the cow moose
ambled off
into the white spruce
the woman
watched
the dead bull moose
so still so long
its black blood
coagulated and the hair
between its toes

turned green. She hadn't noticed
her own face
etched with glass
cuts, her wrists bruised
and the mosquitos. Finally
she brushed her arm
and her own blood
appeared.

WILD STRAWBERRIES

It seems there will always be more deer flies than
          wild strawberries.
Look for them in late June after the wild roses have bloomed.
Like ruffed grouse
they prefer the gravel edges of roads.
Look for the young tall plants to have the bigger berries.
If you sold them, I doubt anyone would, they would have to be
          sold only
by the carat. There never seem to be enough.
Even among the older plants grown too thick, it is almost worth
          stooping over to pick a small solitary
          strawberry
                         you know will close your eyes
and taste like the far-away stars.
What you stoop for may just be a leaf stained red
          as your own fingers. But look:
two more berries under the very leaf.

Rock tripes are lichen, like an old couple

who depend on each other to live

out their black and white lives. Though

neither will ever admit it. He

traipsing all over the rock they live on. She

cooking up greens for eons.

But O how they liked to polka.

BLACK SPRUCE

Beyond the roads
moss, mosquitos, and black spruce
black spruce after black spruce after
black spruce
black spruce straight and tall
long and thin
black-barked with short
stiff blueless green needles, and
apointed crown, if you can call it
that—short-branched and coned
often broken by heavy snows—
and if you can call it a crown
you can say black spruce reign
reign over all of this
reign straight and tall
except maybe an unfortunate seedling
once blocked out of the sun, yet
determined and bent toward its own
light, then a year older
bent back
to live the life
year after year
tall, dark, and narrow
of a black spruce, straight
except for a curved tip
until, at last, claiming its own crown
though ragged
needled, broken
and old (centuries have passed

in the thousand-year bog)
and the right to reign
the right to reign
over all of this—but what kind of a monarchy
is this? black spruce after black spruce
after black spruce
each with its own ragged crown
each in its own right
reigning
reigning straight and tall over all
over all of this
endless bog.

Because in the country once known for its: in
the city once known for its: in the cellar no one
goes down into: rutabagas.

Because once in pasties, mojakka, and hot dishes;
in steel lunch boxes shaped like barns, a thermos
clipped to the loft; on Thursdays at the Blue Note
Café with the special, even then in season only.
Because life was, now isn't without rutabagas.

Because the old holdouts—musk oxen, Tecumseh
and Crazy Horse, narwhals, petrified wood, Joe Hill
and Woody Guthrie—never compromised, and

because the old Finns, the winds, wolves,
coelecanths, Old Believers, boreal owls, and
snapping turtles never gave up.

Because a life is life enough

                              if lived only to taste
the taste of rutabagas.

When the black bear came into the city
at 5 a.m.
when the black bear came into the city
at 5 a.m.
when the black bear came into the city
at 5 a.m.
at Perkins on London Road
when the black bear came into the city
dressed as wedding guest
when the black bear came into the city
at 5 a.m. at Perkins on London Road
it was the longest night of the year
when the black bear came into the city
three of Duluth's policemen
drinking coffee
at 5 a.m. at 5 a.m. at 5 a.m.
at Perkins on London Road
drinking coffee
when the black bear came crashing in
this far into the city
didn't they know?
when the black bear came crashing in
this far into the city
didn't they know?
rushing out into the night
didn't they know?
pistols drawn
didn't they know?
skeletons—*ursus americanus*—have been found

buried with ancient man
didn't they know?
when the black bear came into the city
at 5 a.m. at 5 a.m. at 5 a.m.
didn't they know?
didn't they know?
it was the shortest night of the year
when the black bear came into the city
only to disappear once again into its shadow.
don't we know?

He comes in from the corral made of rough-sawn logs.
His denim shirt, levis faded.
His beard red, fertile as the land it hides
so scarred and rocky you wouldn't want to mow it
      with new machinery.
So hot and humid this Minnesota where in July
the flies are small.
His eyes thin from squinting at the sun welding through
      the haze
as if it needed a hitch

          on the pickup truck. When he
brought
the reindeer from Alberta
they broke out of the trailer at 60 m.p.h. somewhere
in Eastern Montana. Local cowboys said sure
they could roundup three reindeer in no time at all.
It was some time. In fact, it was noon of the next day
when the three reindeer were back in the trailer, their
antlers
broken off

         two hundred thousand years after trees
outgrew the prairie.

The bark of the birch, *Betula*
papyrifera, does not rot, crumble
become obsolete. If buried in the
fall, or even in the Neolithic
bark can be uncovered in the spring
and used: cut into strips
folded and woven into cubes
a treatise inscribed—the root of
zero for example—or lit
to fuel a fire. A birch, *Betula*
papyrifera, log softens soon inside
rots, and becomes
the inevitable earth—nutrients
feeding seeds and basal
sprouts—while the cylinder of bark
remains. Make it into a canister for
wild rice or a snuff box. Birch
Betula papyrifera, bark does not rot
crumble, become obsolete. Birch
Betula papyrifera, bark may peel
rip, even fall off the trunk and
blow away in the wind. Or
as a tattered flap
knock, knock against the trunk
reminding you—as taxes
have been paid in bark and
probability written out on
the bark of the birch
on birch bark. How unthinkable

that probability, that probability of birch bark
written out on birch bark.
How impossible that
written probability, written
on birch bark, knowing
that the bark of the birch
Betula papyrifera, does not die.
That and that
you too
will never go away.

SNAPPING TURTLE

1

One evening after fishing
I lifted the stringer tied to the dock—and
the stringer pulled, pulled
back so I pulled until I pulled up
the stringer of five walleye heads.
I never again tied a stringer
to the dock.

2

Years later on the dock
I saw in the late morning sun
neck out
wrinkled and warted, the head
wedge-shaped with
jaws I knew like a trap (thought
about fingers), turtle, long-clawed
and nasty, old time recluse
I named turtle, turtle
polygram-platted shell the color of mud
and horned like dark mountains
turtle, turtle risen out of muck
out of water, and
now risen up
onto the dock. Now turtle
snapping turtle, said to not bask, snapping turtles
maybe gloat, but not bask in the sun. Yet
turtle, so-named turtle, snapping turtle
on the dock, now

rose up once more
onto thick prereptilian legs, perhaps
a half inch
and clawed
as I walked down to the dock
turtle clawed, turtle clawed to the edge, and
turtle by-no-other-name turtle
bellyflopped off and into
the dark and descending
water. I remember the head
the head--greenstoned,
apocalyptic, and glacial. The head

3

I remembered again
several years later after cleaning fish on the dock
rinsing
fillet after fillet in the water
when
the same jawed and glacial head
pulled a fillet—yikes!
                out of my fingers
and disappeared under the dock.

4

Peering through the dock boards
the kids have seen turtle
though I warned them away
and they stopped swimming
grew up, and moved to different cities.
A mere 25 years have passed and

as much as I remember turtle
turtle remembers. Turtle remembers

when the land was logged, clear cut
except for the alder, right up to
the stream banks. Turtle remembers
when the land was sold, taken back
for taxes, mined, and sold again. Turtle
remembers canoes and beaver pelts.
Turtle remembers iron knives and axes
muskets, and pots. Turtle remembers
priests, robes dark as the tannic water.
Turtle remembers the ones who
came before, the ones who knew what
turtle knew. Turtle remembers
the rivers of ice flowed too far south, broke
off, and melted into lakes. Then all was
green, green as turtle. Turtle remembers.

And as turtle remembers, I remember.
When I clean fish on the dock, I rinse
each fillet carefully
and throw
heads, orts, and skin into the water
and know
though they will soon be gone
not turtle. Not turtle

     5

as once again
           on the dock
that shell olive-drab as a helmet

that ridged and uplifted head
thumb-shaped
but larger like greenstone's thumbs-up
to the Precambrian, snapping turtle—
if not basking, what? dreaming
merely prehistoric dreaming

all afternoon
as the waves washed at the dock
blue sky, foam, and clouds drifted by
and turtle
          on the dock, turtle
may have looked harmless as a Duluth pack
an ax head sticking out, but the serpent
tail and the four clawed legs gave turtle
away. Turtle, old holdout turtle, turtle
island turtle, snapping turtle island turtle
turtle, were you merely dreaming?

Or was I dreaming
as a tiger swallowtail flitted up draft
and down and then
          perched, for a moment
on the sawtoothed mountain top
along the range of turtle's back
          wings pulsing
like a possibility
pulsing, then off again
into the wind.

FOUND IN MY POCKET AFTER WALKING BACK FROM A
PLACE TO BE UNNAMED

Pieces of alder twigs pale
caribou moss brown hairy
as buffalo moss a piece of
birch bark paper with *the
song of the red eyed vireo*
and four notes black rain-
drops on stems jotted down
two pencil stubs a credit
union receipt with the im-
portance of *24 inch cedar
2x4* noted on the back green
fir needles as well as the
scent of green fir needles
and dried to rust fir needles
a leaf bug the size of a green
blueberry two wisp legged
spiders a beetle the size of
a coffee bean a whorl of
delicate tamarack needles
and what else a piece of
greenstone eroded by worry
and imagine too Väinämöinen's
or some other forgotten old
poet's pale green beard hairs.

As September flies into October
the hawks fly south, out of the boreal
forests, out of the arctic, out of
the north, or what we know as north.
The hawks fly south, fly south
until the greatest of the great lakes
Lake Superior leers at them like the head
of a wolf. The wolf leering
cold winds blowing, the hawks veer
down the shore, down the shore of the great lake
hawk after hawk after hawk
flights of hawks flying down the north shore
of Superior
hawk after hawk after hawk
down the head of the lake. Then waiting
waiting for the crossing of the great lake
the hawks gather
circling above
above and before the cold lake
northern goshawk, cooper's hawk, and
sharp-shinned hawk
hawks kettling above
a fine kettling of hawks
stirring overhead
the way my grandmother stirred
her soup, her mojakka with a wooden spoon.
Once when I was a boy
barely tall enough to look into
the dented pot she was stirring, I saw two eyeballs
looking back at me, two eyeballs looking back

at me from the head of a northern pike
swimming in the stirred milk
as my grandmother hummed and tapped
her foot to a minor-keyed hoijakka
and stirred her soup with a wooden spoon.
I will never forget
two eyeballs looking back at me
as my grandmother stirred her soup.
Now the kettle of hawks
circling overhead
stirred by the wind.
Hawk after hawk after hawk
northern harrier, rough-legged and
white-tailed hawk
hawks kettling overhead. The great wind
strumming through the trees as
hawk after hawk after hawk
Swainson's, broad-winged, and red-shouldered
stirred by the wind
kettling over the great wolf's snout
kettling overhead, hawks
waiting for the wind to change
to a major key
for the clouds to lift, then
the hawks rise up
American kestrels, peregrine falcons, and hawks
hawks flying over the head of the wolf
the great thermal lifting their wings out
and over the lake
the hawks flying, the hawks flying south,
south of what we know.

January: the trails of red-backed voles in the snow.

February: the snow letting go, first around the tall pines along the
slope.

March: the geese-flecked sky, sky opened like a geode.

April: male mergansers throwing back their hair like tango dancers.

May: the wink of a twinflower.

June: the brightness that comes into a stone when it is wet.

July: horsetails switching in the wind.

August: thimbleberry stains on your very thumb and forefinger.

September: much to do with rhubarb.

October: deer hair and balsam fir turning gray as the grayest days.

November: unfolding a map in the wind. And the way things
change

December: ice luminaries at solstice melting.

The birch trees are too shy to speak.
They could tell you a thing or two.
How the grasses tap their roots. How
long the summer drought. How wet
the warm whiskered rain. Of course
they love the winter when they hold
the snow, the below-zero cold inside
their bark. No need to complain. No
need for even words. They know
the earth turns, the planets waltz. But
the birch trees are too shy to speak.

There were wolves, still-lived wolves
                    out on the tundra
watching you.
There were wolves, white wolves
against the snow, only their eyes were seen
watching you.
There were wolves in the forest
faces half-hidden
by the trees
                    watching you.
There were wolves, packs of wolves
crossing borders.
There were wolves, black wolves
whose soul was the night.
There were wolves, gray wolves
returning to the desert.
There were wolves, white wolves
returning to the snow.
There were wolves, wolves that left
tracks across the snow.
There were wolves that didn't.

There were wolves, wolves with big teeth
wolves with big eyes
watching you.
There were wolves, wolves leaving
scat.
        There were wolves
black wolves, returning
to the night.
There were wolves, wolves howling

had you listened you would have known
there were wolves.
There were wolves, wolves howling
at the curved blade of the moon.
There were wolves, wolves silent
as they were old.
There were wolves, eyes glaring.
There were wolves
watching you.
There were wolves.

There were wolves
standing on the trail ahead, looking
back at you.
There were wolves. Maybe only one.
only one wolf, a timberwolf
gray and large
large as a life, a life
larger than you ever thought
it could be, larger even
than your own
until you saw
and you knew
there were wolves.

There were wolves before.
There were wolves after.
There were wolves.
There were wolves that shifted like the snow
and turned into ravens
into wind, and back again.
There were wolves.
There were wolves watching you.

¢ TEXT FOR OUR NOMADIC FUTURE

Forest Road 172 takes you
in. Though there are
signs—speed limit 25, trucks
hauling (*ASS* added with black
electrical tape), one lane road
with turn-offs—you must
go. The curves sharp. The tall
white pines lean in. While
the lone raven flying overhead
leads you on
down the gravel road. What
makes you stop makes you stop
at a turnoff. Beside a bog. Though
the picture plants tilt their red
heads and pout. Though
the sundews leave
their leaves liquored up with sunshine.
The sphagnum moss and Labrador tea
draw you in, inviting you
to step, step in
into the cold, cold as Pleistocene
wet you bet to your knees.

GRAY JAY

You might think gray jay is blue-collar
as any Ely guy. Likes to hang around
campsites and from a limb high
in a white pine, swoop down and
grab a crispy piece of fried potato or
beer-battered walleye right off
your metal plate. Or later
swoop down and fish a cigarette
with its beak out of the pack
of Lucky Strikes carelessly left out
on the Duluth Pack. Then
watching gray jay
high up on that limb of that white pine
looking down at the matches
you left out
on a stump, you think gray jay may
need a light after that nice shore lunch
that gray jay is just another good old boy
like you living from day to day. Then
you remember
gray jay doesn't work the mines or cut
trees. That's politics for you: gray as a jay.

To watch a red fox
watch a red fox the way
a red fox watches you.
To watch a red fox
see the agate, not rust, fire
in the eye. Know the fur that
does not move. Know the fur
so stiff, so still. Even the tail
geode tipped. Legs as white
thin as young popple trees.
Long snout peninsulas into
a wet nose black as any
east wind. Mouth as black
the horizon across the snow-
covered lower jaw of autumn. Or
the line across the drum. Ears
triangulated soft fur filters
for frog talk, raven speak
thunder. Eyes fire agate
with black-holed pupils
leading you on
as any hope would do.
The whiskers too
connect. You, if you see
whiskers.

Spruce roots for binding birch bark
            canoes, knife sheaths, snuff boxes, baskets

After peeling spruce roots
I smell the black
under my fingernails
for four days. On the fifth
thunder rolls
in my knuckles and low
in the distance. The rain falls
on the sixth day.
The rain falls like pine trees
reaching down
with their whorled branches and
long green needles.
The rain falls like spruce trees
reaching down into
their roots.   Am I then
rooted to roots
rooted to the land. This land, you might say, I am.

Lay me down on laurel, Labrador tea
      and leatherleaf.

Lay me across sphagnum moss, solomon's seal
      and rosemary.

Gather bladderwort, swamp pinks
      and rose begonias.

Swaddle me in white cedar, black spruce
      and tamarack.

Whisper sweet infinities of juncos, palm warblers
      and Lincoln sparrows. And forever

love me like a bog.

Off Prairie Portage near Basswood Lake
a cedar
four feet in diameter
over a thousand feet of
tangled roots (all those dance lessons
lost) and
over a thousand years old (who would want to
live that long). You can bet
not much to say even then when
one Jacques Cartier paddled by
midlife 1600s
and parlayed a nasal
l'arbor de vie. Cedar maybe
waved a frond. Yet Cartier knew
life on the rocks like life on the bog, the scraggly
the gnarly thousand year future was not
life at the lake, fronds reaching out
to the sun, tapering into the stand-up life. Yet
rot resistant, all the years by lake or bog. Then
used for railroad ties, telephone poles
shingles, fence posts, canoes too. Carpenters
liked the smell. Red squirrels ripped
open the cones, scattered seeds. Deer
browsed the lower branches, hence
the browse line. Swainson's thrush lined
their own nests with
the fibrous bark. When winds tipped
an elder over, a branch
seeking the sun

became a new trunk. Just as you
packsacker, too if you
walk the shapeshifting sphagnum
ground pine, bunchberry carpet
through the sacred cedar woods
and pause
late in the month of May
may you see the calypso, hidden
orchid. May you see.

Before
there were
angels
there were white pines
tall
standing over all
tall
dark barked white pines
with wood
so white, ring after
ring of wood so white it must have been
endless
endless as New England
endless as the Midwest
especially the Upper Midwest
white pines so
endless
who needed angels?
Two hundred feet
tall
white pines
white pines with trunks so thick
two men holding hands
could not reach around to
hold their other hands
men with crosscut saws
and muscle
men who logged
skidded the logs on snow

and ran them down the rivers
after break up
to the sawyers and builders who
built barns and houses
churches even libraries
left clear cuts brush heaps
fire
and a few
a few who remember the ones
who came before
came for the beaver
a few with bark too thick and furrowed
to burn
too far too rocky too steep
a few left standing
tall
over all
a source of seeds and shade
standing tall
I knew a man I knew a man
a man who painted a wooden chair
light blue
and nailed it
high up in a white pine then
he painted a sign
Angel Tree
and set it on the seat of that chair
I don't know what was the matter
with that man
or his wife
she took a step ladder
climbed it every solstice

winter and summer
every equinox
spring and fall
and set a hotdish
on that chair
maybe she had her head in the stars
or was
as knot headed as her old man
or that
white pine
or
maybe not.

Nests low rent in decayed trees
neighborhoods trashed
with wood chips. On-the-ground
feeders
pecking out pine beetles and carpenter ants
with curved surgical clamp flicker bills
and long velcro-tipped tongues.
The black Jack Sparrow mustachioed males
drum roll please, wink and drum along
   all Real Estate ads and
Males Seeking Females classifieds
on hollow limbs until
until female cries out
horsehair bow now scraped over high-pitched
nicelharpa strings
      then
 flies off—white fashion rump and
       yellow flash of wings.
What male can resist?

In the highest dead pine
the immense nest
the immense nest
made of driftwood
beaver sticks, barn
board and hay
so spacious that the grackles
moved right in
like relatives who will
eat the leftovers
the female stiff, surrounded
by are-we-there-yet chicks
in the nest, the immense nest
in the highest dead pine

        while the male away, white with
        black aviator mask
        cruises high, so high
        wings an approximate squiggle
        above the shoreline
        cruises, then
        drops
        drops
        down
        talons, reverse front toe
        and spiculated bottom
        talons extended into
        the splash the size, the shock
        no other news in the world

has broken so, and
rises
talon to salmon
humpbacked
blood hooked talon
to head, other talon to
tail, rises
and flies
flies away with arched wings
bats dream of, spanning six feet.

And I'll tell you straight, back
to the nest, female, chicks.

So tiny, tuftless. You might think
deep in sleep, all day sleep, sleep
thick as spruce.
                    On a limb ragged
brown/white silence of feathers.
Surveillance ears—one set higher, one
lower. And oversized wide eyes.
Sharp short beak. Rag doll on a limb.
All day rag doll on a limb. All day
until the low-lights and the dim-eyed—
mice, voles, tree frogs—ever the slightest
twinge, that moment
when the wild and
the unconscious look into
each other's eyes, then
the short whistling sawblade sharpening
tooth and throat on whetstone
                              sound.

As the story goes, old Italian immigrants
would pour a glass of chianti, put an opera
recording on the Victrola and turn off
the lights. Whether it was the wine or
Puccini or the darkness, tears would flow
down their faces weathered like arid
vineyards. One night alone I poured
a glass of Gabbiano, turned off the lights
and listened. After a few sips of the wine
I heard the arias of the loons, the oldest birds
in the world, played across the lake. Tears
definitely flowed. You could do this experiment
yourself in Isabella, Minnesota. Though
in other locations the results would vary.

Contrary to popular opinion, the American
toad does not have an American flag
stitched to its back like Peter Fonda
in *Easy Rider.* In fact the last American toad
I have seen was green, dark green
Forest Service green, the same green as
my pump, so green I only happened to notice
the slight bulge on the snout of the pump
was a hunkered down toad. When I picked it up
I noticed its belly was desert camouflage
as if ready for assignment to aid the oil-
bearing oppressed. I, however, placed
the toad back on the pump. No call-up today.
Instead, I salute the green, the unnoticed
Easy Rider at home on my pump. Peace, man.

To run with the pack is a cliché. I know. I know too poets aren't supposed to use clichés, though if you read you will notice some do. But to use *to run with the pack* as the title, the beginning of each stanza, and again in the final line could be too clichéd, I was told. I replied that while I used it in the title, I did not use it in every stanza—only in four of the five and in the final line to give emphasis. I thought emphasis was important. More on that later. Beginning the first four lines with *to run with the pack* created an expectation that was broken in the fifth line. Change. Perhaps a welcomed change like the temperature rising above zero, maybe even above freezing, one day in January, and then the following day, of course, plunging back down to dismal normal for the rest of the month. You set the pattern, break it, and return as any good jazz man would do.

    To run with the pack is about wolves, though I realized there were human expectations. The need for emphasis, I thought, was to tell you this poem is about wolves.

    Wolves are large. Believe me if you have never seen one. They do run in packs, large packs of ten or twelve large members. The terror and at the same time the awe of seeing a wolf is difficult to explain. Seeing a pack even more so. And seeing the enormity of a pack of wolves take down a deer is beyond the weight of words. I have watched a pack of wolves from the window of my cabin run down a deer across the snow-covered frozen lake. My cabin is on Lake Mitawan, also spelled *Mitiwan* on the road sign, near Isabella, Minnesota. I don't winter there anymore: too cold, isolated. But I will always see the bloodied tracks leading to the final fury just beyond my ice-locked dock. The larger alpha male ripping off the left rear flank before the female the right, while the others waiting and whimpering for their turn to rip flesh, crush the bones, lick the marrow away. Then after the pack had eaten its fill, ravens moving in to pick up the scraps until all that remained of the bloodied carcass: deer hair, bloodied snow, and the tracks back across the lake and into the thick trees. The wind already blowing the snow filling up the story.

Long after snow melt all that remains of a kill site: deer hair—bones, antlers, hooves, all gone.

My neighbor who overwinters on the lake told me last winter he photographed a kill on the lake. He told me the alpha was larger than any he had ever seen and three-legged. The thought of a pack led by the three-legged enormous wolf ran through my forested mind. How easily our minds turn the natural world into our world.

My neighbor added that he never was able to photograph the ravens: they flew from the remains as soon as he raised his camera.

I wanted to write that just being a wolf and running with the pack is not easy.

Being a wolf is not to be compared with living the human high-end life, best-selling real estate agent or predator on Wall Street running with the rich despite hubris and loss. *To run with the pack* is the flailing hooves or antlers (though antlers are usually shed by midwinter), long run-downs through thick brush and across slush and iced-over lakes, paws clotted, cut, and bleeding. *To run with the pack* as a wolf, a large wolf, though not the largest wolf in the pack or the leader, is fraught with enough difficulty that I didn't want to consider the history or the fate of a three-legged leader, though mishaps with kicking moose, fast cars, illegal traps come to mind.

Therefore, I concluded that *to run with the pack* is not a cliché. It is instead authenticity. How is it that so many would think I wrote a poem titled "To Run With The Pack" in order to write about people? What does that say about our species? Yet I suppose *to run with the pack* is used so much to talk about people that it is a cliché.

But is it a cliché if I am writing about wolves? And if you have ever seen a wolf, a pack, especially a pack take down a deer, how can you not be thinking about wolves?

To run with the pack is not about making large money in real estate even though for real estate you could substitute the word *wilderness*. As more and more wilderness is turned into real estate and sold, then *to run with the pack* could be about the fast lane, money made, and company kept and so easily lost. As so often happens when the stock market crashes, experts focus on the wrong things. Let me redirect you: *to run with the pack* is about wolves.

I suppose then you could also allege that I was trying to use *to run with the pack* as a metaphor. Once it was said that all good poetry is metaphor. Now as style favors the narrower and more direct personal experience, I see no reason to use metaphor. I am merely trying to write what might be the experience of a wolf as part of the pack, part of the natural world often called *wilderness*, at least until it is sold. I suppose it is difficult for most people to see beyond their experience into that of another animal, bird, tree, or any other species. The other is often called *The Wild.*

At this point I have to add that if you were at all inclined to think metaphorically that when it comes to protecting our wild against global warming, climate change, extinction, and all, then we humans are all *running with the pack.* You can look into your own life and as a human capable of thought come to your own conclusions and maybe even react. But I believe the fossil fuel industry, especially those that employ climate-change deniers, bear the burden of blame. Their actions should disgust even our species. I'd rather write about wolves.

However, I did have to consider that *to run with the pack* is a cliché and that I did overuse the phrase.

Thus I drove to the International Wolf Center in nearby (forty miles) Ely, Minnesota. Posted on a wall near the entrance, a map of the area with pinned numbered flags, each number corresponding to an area wolf pack observed and reported to the Center. I knew the range of the packs varied from season to season, from year to year, as did the number of members of each pack (the life of a wolf even at the top of the food chain isn't easy, whether or not this is a cliché). The map was an attempt at identification. I found the flag closest to Lake Mitawan/Mitiwan and the pack that ranged from Isabella to Finland, Minnesota, was pack number 27.

With that information I changed the name of the poem from "To Run With The Pack" to "On Observation Of Pack #27 Southeast Of Isabella, Minnesota, Northwest of Finland, Minnesota, Area Of Relevance." I kept the beginning refrain *to run with the pack* in the first four stanzas, kept the change in the fifth, and returned to *to run with the pack* in the final stanza for emphasis. Cliché or not.

When I wrote "To Run With The Pack" I was writing about wolves. I wanted to use the words for what they were. That you the reader could see the world for what it is. Poetry is, has to be, I think, about the words, the words as they are.

ON OBSERVATION OF PACK #27 SOUTHEAST OF ISABELLA, MINNESOTA, NORTHWEST OF FINLAND, MINNESOTA, AREA OF RELEVANCE

To run with the pack is not only the thrill of the chase
      the barring of the teeth, teeth filleting flesh.

To run with the pack is not only the victory, the takedown
      and afterfeast of loin and offal, breaking bone
      sucking down the marrow.

To run with the pack is to wait. Wait at the end of
      the nomadic chain, alpha male, female, on down.

The pause then to note your pelage slashed to the flesh and
      blood streaked by flailing tines, hip bone bruised or
      broken by kicked up hooves, right front paw pads cut
      frozen blood and snow clumped between.

To run with the pack is to keep up, muzzle bloody and hair
      smacked.

To run with the pack is to keep up.

The tree is, of course, patterned the same
as the entire forest.
As we walked kneedeep
in snow
looking at the tops of fir trees
he said, *There is no perfection*
except imperfection. Yet
we continued looking for a tree without
thin branches, large
gaps between the branches, or branches too long
or too short. Finally
I leaned against the tree that was to be
and shook—the snow falling
off the branches,
onto my coat, and down
my neck. In that snow-flaked light
I bow-sawed through four
frozen inches of fir
until it fell
from the stump. Then, as I held up and examined
the chosen tree
he said, *Don't forget to leave*
one branch to grow back
into the next tree.
As I cut off the other branches, I told him
I once cut two trees
from the same stump. And he told me
I once cut three.

A broken branch
a cry first heard in spring on an empty stomach
ancient as loons
and even before
apostrophed as a red squirrel on a stump
ashamed as the bear who went away upon seeing
      the woman who lifted her skirt
as when frogs first croaked

Barred as an owl
black as a flat tire
blacklisted from a mine
black barred as a three toed woodpecker
blue as a belted kingfisher
built as a boat
burled as two bear cubs high up
      in a pine tree

Collided like rune sleds (aka snowmobiles)
conglomerated as blood
close as the money hiding place
creel smell and your soul to boot
closed as her eyes
cross legged as sitting before a fire
cross threaded

Dark as the step sister sweeping the dance floor
decorated as with spruce boughs, antlers, skull
                                    of a reindeer
delicate as insect parts
dim as walleyed light
dry and resinous as nine pine cones
double bottomed as a lake

Each morning bright as sunrise, sheet ice, or
          spider webs
easy as smoke or falling
                              into a hole
eating its kind
elongated as lint under the unused woodstove
even in midwinter
evening steel sniffing evening

Far out and circumpolar
flat like a raindrop
frightened as a shadow walking in moonlight
flowing as water down from a mountain
                         or coffee into a cup
from the four directions

Gathered together as all of the parts
          even the fur
given mining matters
grimmaced as sure as pointing a finger

Hel with one "l"
hidden like the way back
hissing like the fish
horizontal like the line across the center
howling at a hollow moon
hugged like bears

Imitating a dying person's voice
insect parts inside
inside my swollen ear
in some lakes where the fish especially shy
in the harang of ravens
into a trance
invoked as needed

Just
just as a hand sawing off a limb
just a woman breathing in the closet
just the wind

Kicked back as a wren's tail
                    after it chirps twice
kneeling before three stones
knife hidden in a boot
known as one who killed a bear
        and never let anyone walk behind
known among the three levels
                    kin clan and animal

Lake with no bottom
life to life
like like love
like a chainsaw starting up
living only in otherworldliness
low unwinding howl after howl

Magnetic as sleep
married as to a bear
mesmerizing as any lake or stream
mosquito filled as a dark hole
moonlit clearcut
moose looking place
mother dead with dog
must promise not to talk

Needing only what can pass through
       a brass ring
never this far north, vultures
new world order
no as in no words for
not a man in the corpse
not one to spit on glass and not
       look back
not to be mentioned casually

Of organisms all seeking death
of origins
old as the brother falling down the well

once hard as birch knot
one who must quickly eat a piece of smoked fish
one who turns the eyes
on the drum the map of the dead
out of the mouth of streams

Past on
past on as epic
past on as runes
promised as your sister

Quiet as one who turns the eyes

Rain as the sound of rain falling
              on an oil drum
rather than an old man sobbing
read like a black book
reindeer or raven ridden from the other world
returned as from the dead
rippled as an otter's slide
rivers speaking in tongues

Saved this world by going to the other
snapped like a bra strap
so many fish they had to cut a spruce bough
                  to bring them back
sought after as words
sprinkled as with chewed alder bark

spun to attract prey
starred as the heavens
stomped like the shuttle of a loom
sung as a rune
swooped like a herring gull

Taken as to the top of a hill or
that other place
there where you were told
the sky was perch colored
the soul gets in
thin as a pin cherry
this world too
through the same hole where mosquitos
        get in
tight as a shrink box
toothed like a pike

Very little is known of
virgin birth now illegal

Wandering as the soul
water that supports us
wet as boots walking to the outhouse
where you might see sweet ferns
while waiting for the world to return
who knew the myths best
winked like twinflowers
winter after winter, then glacial hel

wolves that shit black
worshipped like a stone

Xed like sandpiper tracks in the sand

Yet
you as one who concealed
          the nether side of the drum from another's

Zeal.

Late ice turns white, gray, and black
waiting for the red eyes of the loons
                            to come back.

¢ REMEMBERING THE GREAT FIRE 1918

Do you remember when we talked about The Great Fire?
I don't remember talking about The Fire, but I remember The Fire.
You don't remember drinking coffee, eating biscuit, and talking just
        this morning?
What I remember was worse than remembering.
So many who crossed an ocean just for this.

Only the angels led me out of Atumba, all the way to Lawler.

Dreams thrown out like the trash, sparks from a railroad
locomotive
        parched wooded acres.

Where the baseball field now is

                                burnt bodies no one could
identify.

A corpse without an ear, he pleaded with a friend
        to let him die.

So hot and dry
the phone rang, my husband called to fight fire

four miles from our farm. Between this thought and
that thought.

                    I took the eight children, the baby crying on my hip
through the deer paths
hand in hand leading the children but
                                   Edward let go.

I died many deaths for those who died. Senia with so much smoke
in her lungs. I had asked her to sweep the floor

already we could see a ball of flames, death had become
                                   so convincing,
        she said she would never have to sweep that floor
again. She didn't.

When in heaven will I ever see her again?

In the fields of flames we thought we heard a train
through the smoke.

                         On the way to Barnum
a train tipped over on what is now called Dead Man's Curve.

A book of poems was found in the dead man's pocket.

Sparks flying over the house.
The wind picked up. I sat at the table
and cried
            could hardly see the sun. Thus I read from
the book of smoke.

Left behind: a can of tobacco, a clock ticking
the man I would have married.

Because eternity beckoned and I didn't follow. Whatever happened
to the lakes?

They must be angry. As father so often was. So many families
        came, cut down the trees, plowed up the land. Only the rocks
                                                        resisted.

And now. The earth must be tired. Let it rest.

All the roads black corduroy. I even heard the rocks in the rock pile
humming
            the old hymns.

Then came the crows. And I wished I could piss. The sun on the floor
a red blaze. The wind stronger, smelled of smoke.

Seen in the distance, black bodies falling apart. Found on a rock pile.

National Guardsmen began digging graves. Ditches for people buried
beside the railroad.

Three days, no sleep, no food. Only the moon dared to shine
        white, that was before we walked on her.

Flames flew into the culvert, red smoke all around, put the kids
        in the root cellar.

But the door burned. We could only pray.

The wind blew the clothes out of my arms. Who let go
        of his hand?

When the fire jumped the river, blew the horse barn down.

Mother milked the cows, turned the separator, and
        packed the clothes. Only

a wheelbarrow left in a black field. Saved an accordion
        a fiddle and a saw blade.

To postpone our nights. The end without end. While she kept watching
the sky
        sparks flying, thought her dress was tight.

The wind so hard it blew stones against our backs, our faces
        facing a snowstorm of sparks.

Stumps still burning. Black rivers with no bridges.
Trees broken like Verdun.

When the Guardsmen arrived at the scene, they went into
        the cellar and ate.

While the flu epidemic crowded the morgues and the war was over
funerals couldn't wait.

Potatoes and warm bodies in the root cellar. Rutabagas too.

Took a long time to be able to eat cooked meat.

The dead piled up like cordwood behind the Elm Tree Hotel
in Moose Lake.

Devout Christians who denied their children
were ever in the mass graves.   Wrapped blankets around them

and threw buckets of water. Or hid in the well and perished
          longing for the snow to fall

again. A man leading a girl in hand
                              in shock.

All the papers, old books, letters in Finnish
gone. Without clothes or hope or soap.

But left with at least six children and a blind cow. A coat with
two hundred dollars in a pocket
                              across a ditch.

Those whose future turned tax forfeit.
Those identified only by their belt buckles or their shoes.

Mother sat knitting,
told us Dad would put out the fire.

At Coffee Lake two good Norwegians seventy-years-old
caught a man robbing the dead, shot him.

Brushing sparks out of each other's eyes, survived behind
a rock pile in an open field.

Another with several deer in a culvert.

His clothes snagged on the barb wire fence, but he plowed
two furrows.

Wet quilts on us, smoking manure piles, red ball in the sky
                                        dynamite in the barn.
Peat bogs smoldering for weeks.

A hedge of lilacs planted by loving hands that still blooms
beside a foundation.

All our paper money gone, only coins left.

Ten cords of firewood burned, not a stick in the wood box.
A fire in the cook stove could feel so good
                                        in the morning.

 That morning. Smoking ruins, walls. Tongues of flames that
        licked our heels.
                        Two hills burning yet beside the farmstead.

That morning. October 13, 1918. To think we were not dead
in sooted faces, rags of clothes, and doubt
                                        just tired.

Another morning, another red sun over a long black horizon.
Grouse perched on the remains of trees

like it was the dead of winter.

Jim Johnson, a former Duluth Poet Laureate, lived most of his life in Northern Minnesota where he developed an awareness and concern for local culture and history, as well as for the natural world. He has published ten books of poetry and now lives in Cedar Falls, Iowa, and Isabella, Minnesota.

His previous collections include *Text For Our Nomadic Future* (Red Dragonfly Press, 2018), *Yoik* (Red Dragonfly Press, 2015), *The First Day Of Spring In Northern Minnesota* (Red Dragonfly Press, 2012), which won a Northeast Minnesota Book Award and was a finalist for a Minnesota Book Award, and *Driving Gravel Roads* (Red Dragonfly Press, 2009, a collection of fifty prose poems.

In *Selected Poems: One Morning In June* he acknowledges the interconnectedness of our species and plants and animals. In these time of climate change, extinction of species, and increasing catastrophes, we must not ignore the community of plants and animals, as their survival is essential to our own.